# Crabs, Shrimp, & Lobsters

Marine Life
For Young Readers

Text by Stanley L. Swartz

Photography by Robert Yin

Dominie Press, Inc.

Crabs, shrimp, and lobsters have hard shells. They have **jointed** legs. A joint is where two things come together. This is one of the largest groups of animals in the ocean.

◄ **Red coral crab**

Their shell is their home. They **shed** the shell when it is too small. This means the shell falls off. Then they grow a new one that is bigger.

◄ **Hingebeak shrimp**

Crabs and shrimp are **scavengers.**
Scavengers eat things that are dead
and rotten. They eat almost anything.
Lobsters eat live and dead fish.

**◄ Cleaner shrimp**

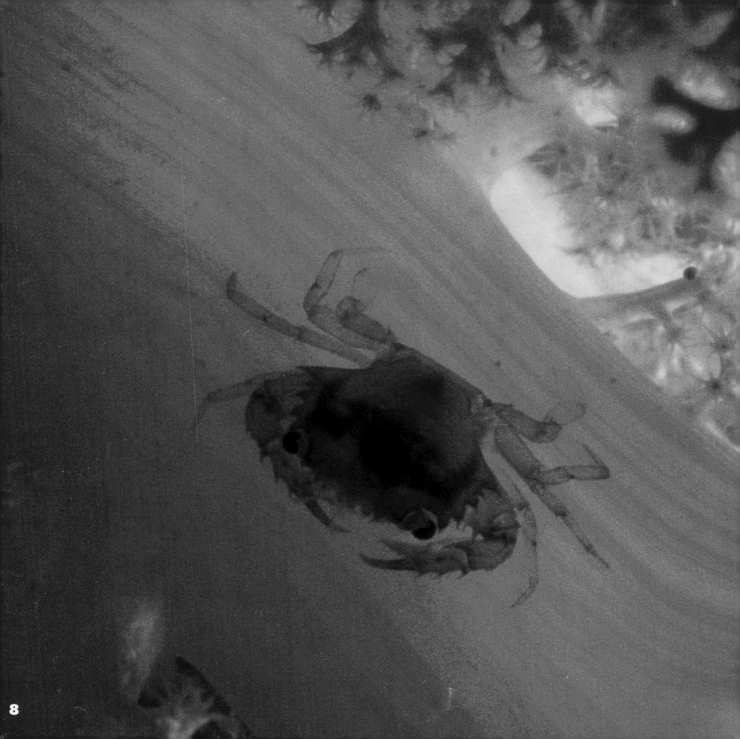

Crabs, shrimp, and lobsters have five **pairs** of legs. A pair is two. If they lose a leg, they can grow a new one. Crabs live in the water and on the land.

◀ **Red pea crab**

Crabs use **tentacles** to feel their way around. Tentacles are like arms. Crabs can live to be six years old. They come in many shapes, sizes, and colors.

◀ **Red spider crab**

The most famous crab is the **Hermit crab.** It gets its name because it likes to hide. The Hermit crab uses another animal's shell. The shell protects the soft parts of its body.

◄ **Hermit crab**

Most shrimp are small and have long bodies. A large shrimp is called a **prawn.** Prawns look just like other shrimp. They can grow to be eight inches long.

◄ **Mantis shrimp**

Shrimp usually swim forward. They can push themselves backward with great speed when **surprised.** Shrimp like warm water, but they also live near Alaska.

◄ **Hingebeak shrimp**

Lobsters have large front legs called **pincers.** Pincers grab and hold things. Lobsters can use these to catch their food. They also use pincers to protect themselves.

◀ **Red reef lobster**

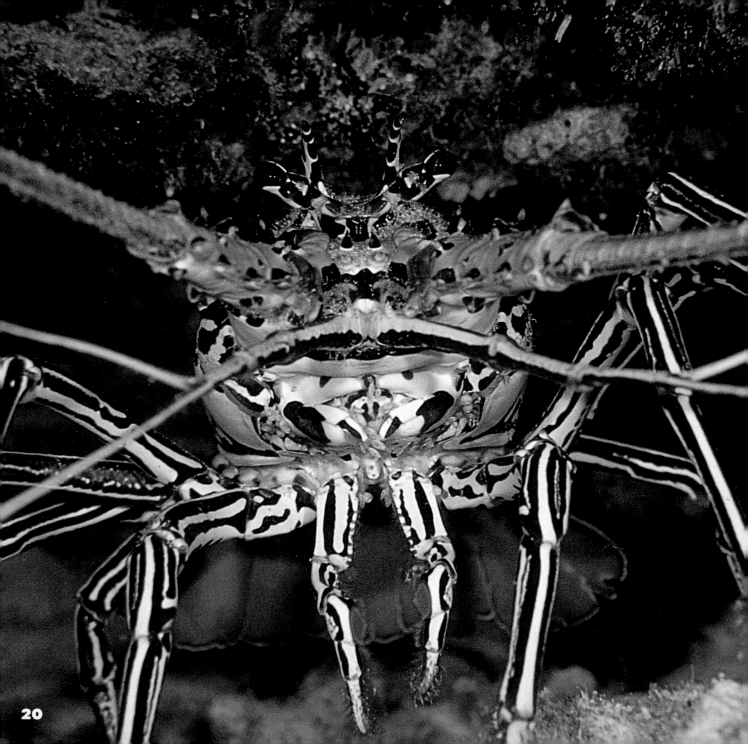

Lobsters live in oceans all over the world. Some lobsters are big and some are small. The **average** lobster is nine inches long. Most lobsters weigh less than 10 pounds.

◄ **Spiny lobster**

Crabs, shrimp, and lobsters are good to eat. Their meat is tender and rich in **protein.** We need protein for our bodies to grow. Crabs, shrimp, and lobsters are a favorite food of many people.

◀ **Porcelain crab**

# Glossary

average: The most common.

Hermit crab: A crab that likes to hide.

jointed: Something that has joints, where two parts come together.

pairs: Sets of two.

pincer: A leg shaped like a jaw.

prawn: A large shrimp.

protein: An important part of our diet.

scavengers: Animals that feed on dead or decaying food.

shed: To lose or fall off.

surprised: Frightened by something that comes without a warning.

tentacles: The part of the mouth used to feel.